# Bob the Preschool Cat

## A BIOGRAPHY OF AN URBAN MANX CAT

*To my friend and colleague Penny Ekamp*
*Best Wishes*
*Romayne*

### E. ROMAYNE HERTWECK

Outkirts Press, Inc.
Denver, Colorado

The opinions expressed in this manuscript are solely the opinions of the author and do not represent the opinions or thoughts of the publisher. The author has represented and warranted full ownership and/or legal right to publish all the materials in this book.

Bob the Preschool Cat
A Biography of an Urban Manx Cat
All Rights Reserved.
Copyright © 2009 E. Romayne Hertweck
V2.0R1.0

Cover Photo © 2009 JupiterImages Corporation. All rights reserved - used with permission.

This book may not be reproduced, transmitted, or stored in whole or in part by any means, including graphic, electronic, or mechanical without the express written consent of the publisher except in the case of brief quotations embodied in critical articles and reviews.

Outskirts Press, Inc.
http://www.outskirtspress.com

ISBN: 978-1-4327-3555-5

Outskirts Press and the "OP" logo are trademarks belonging to Outskirts Press, Inc.

PRINTED IN THE UNITED STATES OF AMERICA

# Acknowledgements

    *A special "thank you" goes to former school teacher Sally Chowning of Branson, Missouri, for reading, rereading, correcting and editing this manuscript. Although she has visited El Camino Preschool, her visit came after Bob's death; therefore her relationship with him has only come about by the printed page. She constantly urged me to publish this book so that others could appreciate Bob's life in the same way she has.*

    *My wife, Dr. Alma Hertweck, was invaluable to me in writing this book. Her expertise in editing, punctuation and, yes, even spelling, was greatly appreciated. An even greater benefit to me was the fact that she spent every day for several years with Bob at the preschool. Her first hand experience with him made it possible for me to tell this story without resorting to fiction.*

# Introduction

The story you are about to read is true. Even the names have NOT been changed to protect the individuals from whatever they need protecting.

There was a cat named Bob. At least that is what we called him. I have no idea what his name was prior to his life at our preschool. You see, Bob was a Manx, a type of domestic cat which has no tail. When he came to the school and adopted us, everyone called him Bobcat and finally, it was shortened to just plain Bob.

Yes, there is a preschool which still exists in Oceanside, California, called El Camino, which my wife and I owned and operated for 20 years. This school is housed in a big ranch style house with extra large rooms and located in the beautiful Fire Mountain area on nearly an acre. In the front are towering, stately date palms and in the back are all types of fruit trees such as apple, plum, avocado and apricot. There is even a macadamia nut tree. This was the home where Bob picked to live – we really had no choice in the matter. It eventually became his school and he was the boss, director, president and CEO (Cat Executive Officer) all rolled into one wonderful cat.

However, Bob was not the first cat to adopt El Camino Preschool as its home, neither was he the last. The first cat lasted only about two or three weeks. Her owner saw her in our front yard as she was driving by and claimed her, then took her home. The second was Bob, which is an incredible story. The third, and last cat, was Smokey whom we eventually brought to our home to live with us.

Smokey did not actually come to the preschool, we came to him. He was a feral cat and starving to death while living in a church parking lot adjacent to the preschool. Staff members told us of this cat, who would eat anything, including lettuce, and slept on the hoods of cars to keep warm. Eventually, my wife, Alma, could stand it no longer. She prepared some food, then went to the parking lot and "snatched him up." He ate the food in large gulps as if he had never seen food before. We looked him over as he ate. He had very little hair on his tail and his little body was just skin and bones. This event taught him where he could find food and afterward he would come to the preschool patio when he was hungry.

In a few weeks, his hair had grown back with a rich gray color. It soon became evident that, unlike Bob, he did not like children. If children came too close, he would run and hide. If they tried to pet him, he would swat at them with his paw. In general, children were just an annoyance which he could not tolerate. Preschools are made for children, not cats, so that meant that he had to go. We took Smokey to our home where he developed into a wonderful companion and followed me where ever I went.

However, this is a book about Bob, not the two other cats, so let's turn our attention to the most remarkable cat I have ever met.

# Chapter 1
## BOB ARRIVES

It was not long after the first cat was claimed by her owner that we discovered the possibility of another cat living at the preschool. There was an old shed at the rear of the back yard, which was really an eyesore. It was filled with all kinds of junk left by the previous owner: doors, parts of a fence, wire, boards and maybe a cat. While we would be contemplating what to do with the junky building we would hear a "meow." However, try as we might, we could not see a cat.

After several days of hearing muffled meows coming from the back of the shed, a healthy-looking, gray cat emerged. He was a Manx with a short stubby tail and very hungry. The El Camino Preschool staff has always had a soft spot for animals, so it goes without saying that this cat was soon fed.

## BOB THE PRESCHOOL CAT

That is all it took, one feeding, for him to start his takeover of the preschool. His first order of business was to find a better place to sleep. That shed was not up to his standards. The preschool building was constructed in increments by one of the former city councilmen as a home for his growing family. As he added on one section of the building at a time, the new roof line would overlap a former roof. This made a space of about two feet which would overhang the other roof. If you were a cat, you could not find a better place to spend the night. It was warm, dry, cozy and, best of all, free from attack by dogs or coyotes. All he had to do was climb the apricot tree, jump on the roof and be safe, dry and warm. What more could a cat want?

By this time, the Manx cat with a bobbed tail was being called Bob. We probably would not have tolerated him had he not shown a great love for children. Adults were OK, but children were what he really liked. They could do no wrong. For example, one day I was looking out of a

## BOB ARRIVES

window while Bob was trying to sleep on the grass. One of our little two-year-old girls decided that she wanted to walk on Bob. You must remember that two-year-olds do not have a great sense of balance. This meant that she had to position herself just right in order to be able to step on him. As soon as she was ready to walk on him, he would move over a few inches. This would require her to "go back to square one" and start her stepping all over again. As soon as she had changed her position so that she could step on him, he would move over a few more inches. Most cats would have just run away. I finally went out and directed her attention to what the other children were doing, thereby saving Bob from getting stepped on.

If two or three children were petting him at once, he was in heaven. He would just flop down wherever he was and let them rub their hands all over him. Life could not get any better.

With his acceptance and love for children, we began to

tolerate his coming into the preschool. We found him to be a well-educated cat who knew everything about everything. For example, chairs were made for cats; couches were made for cats; carpets were made for cats; cubbies were made for cats; baskets were made for cats; desks were made for cats. In fact, everything was made for cats – except brooms.

If a preschool is run like a preschool should be run, it is messy because children can be messy when they are learning new skills. This means that teachers and teacher's aides are constantly cleaning and sweeping in order to keep the school looking half-way decent. The first time Bob was in the school when a teacher picked up a broom, he went flying out of the room. We could only conclude that in his former life cats were chased with brooms. Therefore, brooms were to be feared. I must note that this fear lasted only a short time. Soon a teacher could sweep all around Bob and he would hardly open an eye.

## BOB ARRIVES

An example of how well Bob integrated into the staff and became an absolutely essential member of our community occurred when a parent toured the school prior to enrolling her child. There was, and still is, a certain warm atmosphere in the school environment, which is attractive to most parents. During the 20 years we owned the school, we were always getting offers from people wanting to buy it, since it was unique. Once parents were able to visit and see it in operation, we had to do no selling to get them to enroll.

On this occasion, the parent could not wait to obtain the necessary papers for enrollment after getting a feel for the warm, accepting environment we provided. As she picked up the forms, she remarked that she noticed a cat in the building. "My son is allergic to cats so when he comes to school, you will have to make sure the cat stays outside and away from my son. In addition, when he is out on the playground the teachers will have to make sure the cat is not in the area."

Alma said, "Oh, I am so sorry to hear that your son is allergic to cats. I am sure you would have been happy here as we do provide a rich educational environment. However, we have a good relationship with several quality preschools in the area which do not have cats. I will be happy to provide you with the names, should you desire to visit them."

When Alma told me of the incident, I knew just what she was thinking. "There are many children wanting to come to this school; however, there are many other preschools available, but we have only one Bob. The cat stays."

# BOB THE PRESCHOOL CAT

# Chapter 2
## FEEDING BOB

Most cats eat in order to live, Bob lived in order to eat. His first love was children in the school, but running a close second was food. All my life I have had cats and most all were finicky eaters. The last one we had, Smokey, would snub his food at times, even when I was feeding him his favorite brand. Bob, on the other hand, would eat most anything you gave him and consume all of it before he would quit.

We tried to feed Bob at about the same time each school day which was just after circle time in the morning and between five and six in the evening. However, preschools being as they are, things never always run on schedule. A child may bump his/her knee and require a band-aid. Should there be a drop or two of blood, in addition to the band-aid, the child would require some lap-sitting and hugs. In the event

## BOB THE PRESCHOOL CAT

that the child had a fever or upset stomach, more time was required and feeding cats could wait. Children always took precedent over cats when injuries occurred.

With this in mind, I was not surprised to arrive one morning after ten and have Bob meet me in the parking lot with a tale of woe. He really put up a howl. It was obvious that somehow his feeding had been missed. He followed me all the way to the preschool yelping, howling and meowing telling me that he had not been fed and that he was starving to death. To hear him tell it, he was dying of hunger and could not wait another minute.

I went straight to the pantry and obtained a can of cat food, which I put in his bowl and took it and Bob to the patio. Bob could hardly wait. He started eating large gulps of food and in a very short time all the cat food was gone and he was licking the dish and finally licking his lips. I was just amazed that he could eat so fast, but I guess when people are very hungry they can bolt down their food also.

## FEEDING BOB

I walked into the office and told Jill, the administrative assistant, that Bob had told me how she had failed. Jill was doing the morning attendance records so she hardly looked up when she said, "How come?"

I told her that Bob said that she had forgotten to feed him and that he was starving to death. I proceeded to describe how hungry he was and how he just gulped down his food.

Jill looked up and said, "You realize, don't you, that Bob lies. You have been suckered. I fed Bob at nine this morning and he just conned a second can of cat food out of you. You were taken in by that cat."

## BOB THE PRESCHOOL CAT

That taught me to always ask before feeding Bob since he would always pretend to need food, regardless of when he had been fed.

There was no problem feeding Bob during school days. However, weekends were a different matter. On Saturday and Sunday I would come by the school in the morning and give him a can of food. But feeding him in the evening always seemed to slip my mind, especially during the winter months when it became dark at an early hour.

Many evenings I would come to the school when it was dark and Bob had already climbed on the roof to sleep. After getting him a dish of dry cat food, I would call him, "Here Bob. Here Bob."

He would always answer at once, "Meow." (Which I assumed to be "Here I am" in cat language.) After one or two meows, he would amble over to the edge of the roof and look down at me.

The kitchen at the El Camino Preschool has a small porch which is high enough to be close to the roof. Many

## FEEDING BOB

times I would obtain a ladder from the kitchen and reach up, grab Bob and place him near his food. Sometimes Bob had other ideas; he wanted to tease me. As I would reach for him, he would jump back. As soon as I backed away, he would once again come to the edge of the roof, only to retreat as soon as I tried to grab him.

Finally, I would just give up and say, "OK , you silly cat, I am leaving and you can just starve." I would then take the small ladder in the school and prepare to leave.

The kitchen was on the west side of the school and the apricot tree, where he climbed to the roof, was located on the east side. As soon as Bob would see me go in the school, he would scamper across the roof, down the apricot tree and run around the building as fast as he could go ready to eat. Teasing me was fun, but when it might cost him a meal, he was in no mood for playing games.

At this time we had two preschools. One was located on the east side of Oceanside and Bob's school was located on the west. Oceanside Boulevard was a direct way to travel between the two schools. One day as I was coming back to Bob's school, I stopped at Longs Drug Store, which is located on Oceanside Boulevard near College Boulevard. To my amazement and delight, there was a stack of tuna fish cat food near the check-out counter. It was listed as a manager's special – six cans for a dollar.

Tuna fish was Bob's favorite food so I asked the clerk if it was any good. I was told that it was very good cat food and that they had no complaints. I then purchased $10.00 worth. It does not take a mathematician to figure out that this would be 60 cans, which would last about two months. Bob was fed canned cat food in the morning and dry cat food in the evening.

When I got to the school, we opened a can and let Bob see what he thought. Most tuna is either packed in oil or water. This was packed rather dry; which was just the way Bob liked it. He couldn't have been happier.

During the time we owned and operated the preschool, I was a full-time professor at MiraCosta College. One day, two months later after I had finished teaching my nine o'clock class and walked into my office, the phone rang. It was Jill telling me that she had forgotten to mention that Bob ate the last of the tuna yesterday and that they had to feed him dry cat food this morning. She went on to say that, "Bob is not a happy camper."

I asked my secretary at the college if I had any appointments that morning and she said, "No." I then told Jill I would leave and buy Bob some food.

There were two supermarkets on Oceanside Boulevard near the preschool. I went into one (which will remain nameless) and looked over the available cat food. They were also having a sale on cat food – five for a dollar – and it was fish. (Just how lucky could I get?) I reasoned, "Tuna is fish so Bob would probably like this just as well." I had forgotten what I had learned in my college logic course, or I would have known better. *All Tuna are fish, but all fish are not Tuna.* There was something that worried me about the five for a dollar fish cat food. First, it was not a name brand and, second, it had a generic white label which said only FISH. I did not purchase $10.00 worth, like I did the tuna at Longs Drug Store. I was a big spender, however. I got three cans, which cost a total of 60 cents plus tax.

As soon as I got to the preschool, I found a dish, opened a can of FISH and presented it to Bob. He came jumping for joy, until he was about two feet from the FISH dish. He stopped and every hair on his body stood up. His eyes got wide and he arched his back, then he gingerly approached the dish. One sniff of the FISH and he

## FEEDING BOB

was gone – out the door, down the side of the school and in the front door. He then went on a "Holy Tear" jumping from chairs to tables to cubbies to record players, then around and around the pre-kindergarten room. Bob was not in the best physical shape, and I considered him to be a very lazy cat, so after several circles around the room, he was out of breath and stood there panting, all the while glaring at me and Jill. It was like he was saying, "How could you do this to me? Do you expect me to eat that slop?"

I turned to Jill and said, "I think I am going to make another trip to the supermarket."

Jill asked, "What do you want me to do with the FISH cat food?"

I told her to just toss it and that I would buy some name brand cat food like Friskies. When I returned with some "decent" cat food, Bob slowly approached the feeding dish and sniffed it before starting to eat. He did, true to form, eat every bit and then licked the dish clean before licking his lips.

# Chapter 3
## EVERY DAY IS DIFFERENT

Since Bob was now in control of the preschool, he felt he could do exactly as he wished. The first organized activity of the day in each classroom was "circle time." During this period the teacher would read a story and have some songs, or other group activity, prior to the regular classroom activities. Bob loved circle time. When the teachers first informed me that he was joining in the circle, I thought they were kidding me. I knew that Bob was involved in the school activities, but being a part of circle time – no way!

I made it a point to be on hand one day when classes started so I could watch what Bob did. When the teacher called the children for the circle, they all came and sat on the carpet. I looked up and here came Bob and took his place in the center of the circle. I was told that sometimes he would try to sit between two children in order to obtain both of their attentions. Teachers frowned on his sitting beside the children since they would pay more attention to Bob than to circle activities; therefore, he soon learned that if he wanted to be part of circle time, his place was in the middle. He would normally lie on the carpet until circle time was over and then amble up to the office to look for a place to sleep.

He soon discovered that there were many delightful places for a cat to sleep. Jill, our administrative assistant, was very tolerant of his activities – probably too tolerant. Bob could be found sleeping in the in-basket on her desk, on the copy machine, beside the copy machine, in the middle of her desk, on her lap and, of all places, between her and the back of her office chair.

This last location took some ingenuity on his part. First, he would jump on Jill's desk, he would then jump on the arm of her office chair. As soon as he had a firm footing on the chair arm, he would climb up between her back and the back of the chair. Once in this position, he would start to wiggle and squirm until Jill would move forward a little. He would keep up the wiggling and squirming until Jill would move far enough forward to give him a large enough spot to sleep. This meant that Jill would sometimes be sitting on only the very front of the office chair while Bob was having a wonderful nap.

One day, Alma was sitting in the business office, (not to be confused with the school office) when Rita, one of our teachers, burst in and pretended to be very upset. "I quit!" she said.

Alma said, "What's wrong, Rita?"

Rita said, "Wasn't my assignment this morning to greet the parents and children? Well, one of the staff members has taken over my job without saying one word to me. Come and see for yourself."

Alma and Rita walked to the front door and just then Bob was seen escorting a parent and her child to the school. As soon as they got to the door he was back out to the parking lot to greet the next parent and her child or children. Of course, the children just loved it and Bob received a lot of petting as he walked them to the front door.

I don't want to leave the impression that Bob did this every morning. He was basically a lazy cat and greeting all the cars with all the children took too much energy. He soon discovered that he could receive the same amount of attention just by "hanging around" the front door while children were arriving. He would usually sit out in the front and wait for the children until it was circle time

One morning about five o'clock, the phone rang by my bed. I answered, "Hello."

The other party said, "Is this Dr. Hertweck?"

I said, "Yes, it is."

"This is the alarm company. There has been an intrusion at the El Camino Preschool. It looks like the break-in is located in the pre-kindergarten room. The police have been notified and are on their way. They have requested for you to come and unlock the building so they can make a search," the speaker said.

I quickly dressed and rushed to the school. Sure enough, there were two police cars in the parking lot. When I arrived, they had already made a preliminary search of the grounds and had found no point of entry. I was asked to unlock the front door so they could search for the intruder.

I told them. "Before you begin your search, I must turn off the alarm system."

The policeman in charge said, "No way. We can't let you in the building until we determine no one is there. It is just too dangerous."

I said, "Do you really want to go in there and once again set off the alarm? Do you realize that we have three sirens which are so loud they could 'wake up the dead.' The one outside is so loud that it can be heard more than a block away. I am sure that the neighbors would not appreciate being awakened again."

After a consultation, it was decided that I would unlock the door and turn on the lights. The police would then enter and wait until I had disarmed the alarm system. I promised to stay by the front door until the building was completely searched.

All went according to plan until the police searched the pre-kindergarten room. I heard them yell, "We found the intruder."

When I came into the room I saw Bob standing in the middle of the floor, completely traumatized. Every hair was standing straight up and his eyes were wide with fear. He had never heard anything as frightening as the three sirens. I rushed over and picked him up while the police were having a good chuckle. I tried my best to calm him down as we turned off the lights, reset the alarm and locked the door. Once outside, the police left and I stayed a while to comfort Bob until I felt he was back to a semi-normal condition.

It goes without saying that we admonished the janitorial staff to never again turn on the alarm and lock the door before making sure that Bob was outside.

One day Deanie, our Kindergarten teacher, came to me and suggested that Bob might need a bath. She felt there was a good possibility that he had fleas. I told her that I had never given a cat a bath and at my age, I was too old to learn. She said it was no problem and if I would purchase some flea soap and a flea comb she would be glad to bathe Bob. In fact, she suggested that we might make it a class project and let the children in her class help.

The more I thought about having the children assist in Bob's bath, the more I liked the idea. I went to the pet store and purchased the necessary items and gave them to Deanie. She said Bob would receive a bath on the next warm day.

When the warm day arrived, Bob got his bath on schedule. I asked Deanie how things went and she said, "Great. Bob cried a little but with the children present, he calmed down and made it easy for all involved."

That afternoon when I came over from the college, Bob was all dry and fluffy. Interestingly, he was in a very good mood and no worse for the wear of taking a bath.

Bob considered himself to be the mighty hunter. There were, and still are, many gophers at the preschool. Some of the gophers have lost their fear of humans now that Bob is no longer present. When he was there, you could see him sitting by a gopher hole for hours at a time. However, I never had any indication that he ever caught one.

This is not to say that his hunting was limited to gophers. We found bird feathers in the yard from time to time, which seemed to tell us that bird hunting was more successful than gopher hunting.

One day, to a teacher's horror, Bob brought a live bird to a classroom window and pressed it against the glass. He desperately wanted the children to see his catch. Since the bird was still alive, one of the teachers ran outside and made Bob release the bird. Once free, the bird ran a short distance then started flying. We were thankful that the bird was not severely injured.

Another day I heard one of the teachers yelling, "Come quick……..there is a snake in the yard."

We have had several snakes visit the preschool and since they are not a dangerous variety, we just escort them out of the area. This time Bob knew something was amiss, so he got to the snake a little before I did. When I arrived, he was having a lot of fun with the snake. He was batting it with one paw and then with the other. Someone was quick enough to think of a camera. It was loaded with black and white film and gave us a good record of Bob's prowess with snakes. Finally, someone had to pick Bob up and hold him while I herded the snake out of the yard.

When Alma and I decided to open a preschool, we had to devise a plan which would allow each to share in the responsibilities. Alma was to be in charge of the daily activities and work with teachers, parents and children. I, on the other hand, would work behind the scenes and keep the books, write the checks for bills, make deposits etc. In general she would be the glue to hold the school together and I would be the oil to keep the wheels turning.

# EVERY DAY IS DIFFERENT

My work did not depend on my being at the school at a specific time. It was much better for me to go over to the school and work on the books or record tuition payments when no one was around. It was always kind of eerie to be alone in the large school with not a sound to be heard. Suddenly one night there was a WHAM, BANG, BANG on the front door. Needless to say, I was startled.

The front door to the business office is solid wood, which opens inward and was constructed by one of our student's father. Also, there is a security screen door which opens outward. At the sound of the banging, I opened the wooden door and found Bob sitting outside the screen door looking wistfully like, "Well, are you going to let me in?"

Bob had put his claws in the holes in the screen door and rather shook it so that the sound was like someone knocking. After his first success in letting me know he wanted in, whenever I was working late, he would rattle the screen so I would admit him to the office.

Once inside, he would start looking for a place to rest.

## BOB THE PRESCHOOL CAT

If I were not too busy, I would find a brown paper sack and put it on the floor. Bob would crawl in the paper sack and sleep until I was ready to leave. However, should I be very busy and not have time to search for a paper sack, he was on his own. Then he would sleep on a chair, the copy machine, a desk or any other place fit for a privileged cat.

I did get very disgusted with him one time when I let him share the office with me. He had just banged on the screen door for me to let him in and as soon as he was inside, he coughed up a hairball on the carpet. My thinking was, "Why not rid yourself of the hairball prior to asking to come in the office?" I guess I will never understand cats.

# Chapter 4
## THE INJURED PAW

As a full-time professor, my mornings and much of the afternoons were spent at the college rather than at the preschool. I had just finished teaching my nine o'clock class and had settled down in my office to get some work done when the phone rang. It was my wife, Alma, wanting to know how busy I was. I told her it was just the usual stuff – not too involved or pressing.

She then told me that when she arrived at the preschool, there were bloody paw prints on the patio and that Bob had a cut on his left front paw. They had cleaned up the bloody paw prints and she had a bandage on his foot to stop the bleeding. However, she said that it looked pretty bad and maybe I should take a look at it.

I told my secretary, Dolores, that there was a problem at the preschool and I needed to take care of it. I would be back for my noon class and if any students needed to see me, I would meet with them at 1:00.

When I arrived, Bob was sitting on Alma's lap with his left front paw all wrapped up. I took off the bandage and looked to find what seemed to be a deep cut in the center of his pad. I told Alma, "I don't like the looks of this. I doubt if it can be stitched, but we can't leave it this way. I think I better call Dr. Brust at the Oceanside Veterinary Hospital."

Dr. Brust was a neighbor of ours and lived a few doors to the north. When I call the animal hospital I never know if he will be available. You see, Dr. Brust specialized in treating large animals, like horses, and he made house calls or to be politically correct, I should say barn calls. It was very lucky for us that Dr. Brust was in the office and I soon had him on the phone.

"Don, this is Romayne. We have a problem with our preschool cat. Bob has a very bad cut in the center of his left paw, right in the pad. It looks pretty deep. We have the bleeding stopped. What should we do?"

Dr. Brust said, "If you think it is very deep, you better bring him in. I will wait for you if you can bring him in right now."

I told Alma that Don wanted us to bring Bob to the hospital right now. However, we didn't have a cat carrier and we had never taken Bob anywhere in the car, so I had no idea how he would react. Some cats I have had just freaked out if you took them in a car. I asked her if she thought she could hold him while I drove down to the San Ruis Rey Valley. Alma said that she thought it would be no problem. Alma was right. When we got in the car, Bob just snuggled down on her lap and rode that way until we arrived at the hospital. I carried Bob into the hospital and told the woman at the desk that I had just talked to Dr. Brust and he wanted to see Bob now.

## THE INJURED PAW

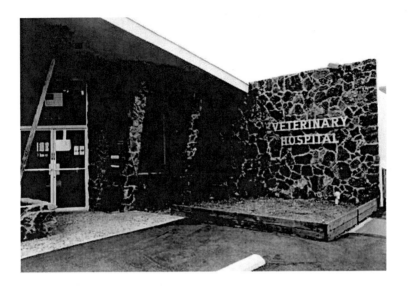

She said, "Of course, take Bob into the first examining room on your right." I thought to myself, what wonderful treatment. I just wish that humans could get this type of consideration when they go to their doctors.

Bob was not too happy in the examining room. There were strange smells and the table where I placed him was cold stainless steel. Both Alma and I tried to comfort Bob, since he was getting a little restless and showing some anxiety. By the time we had him settled down a little, Dr. Brust came in and said, "Well, well, well. Bob what have you done to your paw?" He turned to me and said, "I want you to hold his head very tightly while I examine the cut. Animals can bite if they are hurt and this may hurt a little."

Bob squirmed a little, but did not make any attempt to bite while he was being examined. After looking at the wound, Dr. Brust turned to me and said, "You were right, it is pretty deep. I will cleanse the cut the best I can, but you will never know if anything is up in his paw which can cause an infection. This means I will give him a shot and you will have to give him antibiotics until the wound heals."

I immediately thought of the many times I had to put pills down a dog's throat. I really got pretty good at it. I would open the dog's mouth and place the pill back in the mouth, then hold the muzzle shut until he swallowed. I didn't think I wanted to do this to a cat. I said, "Don, if you think I am going to put my finger down that cat's throat you have got to be crazy."

Dr. Brust started laughing at me. He said, "I gather from that remark that you have never given a cat antibiotics."

I said, "You are right and I am not going to start now."

Dr. Brust said, "Giving him his medicine is the least of your problems. I will prescribe a liquid antibiotic which Bob will love and he will beg for more."

Then Dr. Brust turned to Alma and me and asked, "Where does Bob spend the night – inside or outside?"

We told him outside, since he would set off the burglar alarm if he were left to roam the school all night long.

Dr. Brust then said, "Until his paw heals, Bob will be very vulnerable. He cannot run very fast and in no way can he climb a tree with a bandage on his paw. I doubt if you will have a problem in the daylight hours with all the activity at the school, but at night with all the coyotes running around, he could become a good meal. You will have to keep him confined all night long until he can go without a bandage."

After Dr. Brust cleansed the wound, gave him a shot and placed a neat bandage on his paw, we were almost ready to return to the preschool. I paid the bill while Dr. Brust obtained the antibiotics and a feeding tube. He also gave us instructions on the care of the injury and how long

## THE INJURED PAW

we could expect it to be before it healed.

As we returned from the San Luis Rey Valley to the preschool, Alma and I discussed what in the world we were going to do to keep this cat confined at night. We had a good reputation for having a super clean preschool. Many people had remarked that it really smelled good. (I always wondered what other preschools smelled like.) To keep up our reputation, the school had to be cleaned thoroughly each and every night. This cleaning generally took about three hours. During this time, the doors were left open as the cleaning people went in and out of the school.

Since there was no way we could use a classroom, we finally decided to let Bob sleep in the staff bathroom. We would inform the cleaning staff that under no circumstances were they to open and clean the bathroom. Every morning, a staff member would be assigned the task of cleaning and sanitizing the room prior to the start of the school day.

All this required that we obtain a litter box for Bob and some cat litter. We also placed a bowl of water and a nice blanket for his bed in the room. After all, he would be confined in the staff bath for about thirteen hours each night, from 6:00 PM to 7:00 AM.

The next day it was time to start Bob on his antibiotic treatment. I filled the feeding tube up to the mark with the thick liquid. The idea behind the feeding tube is that it would be gravity fed and as the cat licked the bottom, more liquid would be available. Alma picked Bob up and placed him on her lap in the same position that Bucky Katt sits in the comic strip, *Get Fuzzy*. In this position Bob was placed in a vertical up-right position with his hind feet on her lap and his face and front paws facing outward.

Bob held out his injured paw as if to say, "Look at my

sore paw." I brought the feeding tube down near his mouth to let him sniff it. He immediately began to lick the tube very energetically until all the liquid was consumed. As he was licking his lips, he looked up as if to say, "Well, how about some more."

Our next task was to place hot moist packs on his paw before giving him a clean bandage. Alma and I rather worried how he would react when we actually started touching his injury. We really had nothing to worry about. As Bob was sitting in the *Bucky Katt* position, he just held out his paw and seemed to enjoy the hot packs. It could have been that he enjoyed all the attention in addition to the moist heat feeling good. Whatever the reason, our bedside manner, the extra attention or the luxury of the moist hot packs, Bob was a wonderful patient.

Bob soon learned that having an injured paw was not all bad. He found from our caring for him that all he had to do to obtain attention was to hold out his bandaged paw and

## THE INJURED PAW

someone would give him a stroke or two.

He would now go down to the classrooms and hold out his paw while at the same time giving a pitiful meow. This would bring instant attention and love. Several children would drop whatever they were doing and rush over to pet Bob. He also found that it worked even better on parents. When it was time for the children to be picked up, Bob would be down by the entrance showing off his bandaged paw while giving that now famous pitiful meow. Reactions like, "Oh, you poor cat," along with some petting just delighted him.

All good things must come to an end. Bob's paw eventually got well and we no longer had to keep a bandage on it. Holding out his paw with no bandage on it did not invoke sympathy no matter how much he meowed. There was only one thing left to do and that was return to his role as the number one preschool cat.

# Chapter 5
## SPECIAL DAYS

A quality preschool such as El Camino, does more than "warehouse" children while their parents work. It is a vibrant, active, exciting world where children can learn, grow and develop social skills to last a lifetime.

In order to provide such an environment, a different theme was designated for each week. In addition, all holidays were given special treatment to help the students appreciate our history and our culture. Bob, as you will see in this chapter, always took an active role in these events.

**Bob Week**

One week during the fall was designated "Pet Week." We taught children how pets can and do occupy an important place in many families. Children were encouraged to bring their pets for "show and tell," provided that pets, other than cats or dogs, were caged. It was not unusual for children to bring snakes, birds, fish, puppies and hamsters.

Since Bob was the school's pet, one year we not only called it Pet Week, but also Bob Week. For this occurrence we had T-shirts made with a line drawing of Bob printed on them. The shirts were light yellow with black and gray printing. To make it possible for each and every child to participate, we sold them below cost at $5.00 each. These were top quality shirts which normally sell in the specialty shops for many times more. Bob was such a part of the everyday experience that each child felt he/she must have a Bob shirt. Parents were wheedled into buying at least one. Once the child had a Bob Shirt, it was difficult to separate child from shirt. In fact, I was told that

## SPECIAL DAYS

some children even slept in them.

An unexpected twist to the Bob T-shirt promotion came when a parent asked if we could have large adult shirts made? It seems that her son and a group of his friends had grown up together and were now in high school. They wanted to have an identity all their own which was different from gangs or special interest groups at the school. First, they wanted to adopt Bob as their mascot. Second, they needed T-shirts with Bob's likeness on them so it would give them identity. My reaction was, "Sure, why not?"

These were very large boys I found out. I ordered a dozen Bob shirts with half being adult large and the other half being extra large. The printing was the same as for the preschool students with the El Camino Logo and Bob's picture printed on a yellow shirt with black ink. I figured that this would be wonderful advertising, so I also sold these below our cost. When all was said and done, we sold eleven of the twelve shirts to high school students. I have always wondered what the reaction was when these guys first walked into a high school classroom wearing El Camino Preschool T-shirts. When I noted their size, I doubted that very many, if any, snide remarks were made to their faces.

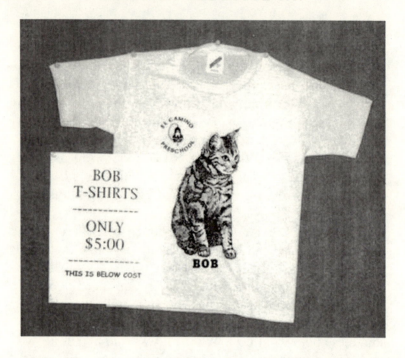

## Halloween

Of all the fall events, other than Christmas, Halloween was Bob's favorite. Each year we constructed a pumpkin patch with over 100 pumpkins, which would have made Charlie Brown proud. This was the original "sincere" pumpkin patch for which Charlie dreamed. It was complete with scarecrows, ghosts, corn shocks, spiders and bales of hay. On October 31, each class was provided a picnic snack in the pumpkin patch. At the end of the picnic, each child was able to select his/her own pumpkin to take home and carve. The only restriction was that the child must be able to carry his/her pumpkin. That way, the smaller children got small pumpkins and the larger and older ones were able to carry bigger pumpkins.

## SPECIAL DAYS

As the pumpkin patch was being created, Bob would follow us around and as soon as the corn shocks were made, he was in his element. He would immediately crawl inside one of the corn shocks and make himself a bed. During the picnics, he would wander around to see what was happening. Prior to Halloween, the teachers would make costumes for Bob, which he would wear while making his rounds visiting all the children. Sometimes this was just too much for a cat to endure, so he would return to his corn shock bed and take a nap while the costumed children finished their picnic.

## Christmas

(This was Bob's favorite time of the year, and we will devote the entire next chapter to his activities at that time.)

## Mother's Day

Mother's Day was celebrated with a Mother's Day Tea. (It was suggested that we call it Mother's Day Punch since very few ever drank tea.) During Bob's lifetime, we set up tables in the front yard or in the classrooms so that mothers and children could sit together. Bob would be "dressed up" with a pink ribbon and bow around his neck. He played the part of the perfect host. He would go around from table to table giving each a welcome and, of course, hoping that someone would pet him in the process.

**Father's Day**

Unlike Mother's Day, there was nothing formal about the way we celebrated Father's day. Each dad was requested to bring a blanket and sit on the front lawn and eat hamburgers and French fries with his child or children. We purchased the food from Burger King, which catered the event each year for nearly twenty years. Each year between fifty and one hundred dads would take off from work to share this time with their children.

From Bob's perspective, this was much better than Mother's Day since everyone was on the ground at his level and he did not have to get "dressed up" for the occasion. He took full advantage of his position by going from child to child looking for some recognition and a little petting. Dads were only tolerated since most do not give cats the respect that cats desire.

It is interesting to note that even though eating was Bob's favorite activity, he never begged for food when the children were eating. There were always hamburgers and fries left over after the Father's Day Picnic, but Bob was too much of a gentleman cat to ask for his share of human food. Cat food was a different matter and he did not mind doing a little begging for it.

A comic event took place one year when the wind was blowing and a child released a hamburger wrapper. It blew toward Bob and landed squarely on his face while he was resting on the grass. Being a very "laid back" cat, he just lay there with the wrapper covering his face until a child removed the wrapper.

## Graduation

At the end of June, a graduation ceremony was held on the front lawn. The parents would gather under the palm trees while waiting to see their children perform. After marching out of the school to their designated spot, the children would sing and receive their diplomas.

Bob had no desire to be with the parents. He was always inside with the graduating class as they were getting "dressed" and preparing for the ceremony. One of the teachers suggested that since Bob wanted to be with the graduates, why not make him a hat and let him be part of the activities? My reaction was, "Yeah, sure. How are you going to get a cat to wear a hat and stay with the children during the graduation ceremony?"

I had to eat my words. Not only did Bob gladly wear his graduation hat, but he walked out with the children and promptly found himself a place in front of everyone. It would have made a nice story if I could have said that he got up and sat on a chair like the children. He did not. What he did was walk out with the graduates and lie down on the grass in front of the children, all the time wearing his hat. He stayed in that spot and did not move until the close of the graduation ceremony.

# BOB THE PRESCHOOL CAT

# Chapter 6
## CHRISTMAS

Bob enjoyed all of the special days at the preschool. However, none could compare with his delight of being part of the activities during December. We kicked off the holiday season with Teddy Bear Night during the first week of the month. This meant that the Friday following Thanksgiving, we were at the school decorating and preparing for the dozens of people who would be in attendance.

Every year we clipped great quantities of evergreen boughs and brought them to the school. These were placed all over the building, in windows surrounding candles (unlit, of course) and across the mantle of the huge fireplace. We added poinsettias and pine cones to make it a really festive scene. Of course, every room had a Christmas tree.

As soon as I started carrying in the boxes containing the

artificial Christmas trees, Bob was on hand to "supervise." (At least that is what one of our teachers called Bob's interest in our activities.) I always started assembling the Christmas trees in the pre-kindergarten classroom, which happened to be one of Bob's favorite places. As I was putting each part of the tree in place, he would sit and watch me intently. As soon as the tree was completed, he would stake out his spot under the tree where he would sleep for the next three weeks. When the teachers placed fake presents under the tree, Bob would just move over to make room for the boxes or he would move in front of them. There was no way he was about to leave his spot under the tree – he was there first.

As soon as the tree was decorated, he would play with any ornaments which he could reach. To his credit, we

## CHRISTMAS

never found any damage to our decorations above the "Bob line." He did, however, give the balls hanging on the low branches a good "swat" now and then. When the teachers discovered that he liked to play with the ornaments, they hung some that would be OK for Bob to play with. His favorites were satin balls which would unravel a bit.

Our holiday activities at the preschool lasted three or more weeks. The first event was Teddy Bear Night, which was held the first week in December. For this night, the pre-kindergarten classroom was decorated with lots and lots of bears: stuffed bears, printed bears and on a long shelf in the entry there were 14 bears holding letters which spelled out "Merry Christmas." We always started the event at 7:00 PM and promised the parents we would conclude at 8:00 PM. This was so the children could attend and still get a good night's rest. In addition, we asked that everyone come in his/her pajamas. Children were also requested to bring a favorite Teddy Bear.

Each evening, Bob would go outside and sit on the steps as soon as the school closed. On Teddy Bear Night, the school did not close. At five o'clock, things really started "humming." The janitorial staff worked feverishly to get the school sparkling clean by 7:00 PM. Teachers moved most of the equipment out of the pre-kindergarten classroom in order to make room for the large amount of people who would be attending. My job was to make lots and lots of coffee. Alma was busy making her favorite fruit punch and arranging tons and tons of cookies on platters. Bob made it his job to supervise each and every activity. He was all over the place from the kitchen to the classrooms to the outside and back again. He knew something big was about to happen and he wanted to be in the middle of it.

Normally the schedule was pretty tight, since we promised the parents that the activities would not last beyond 8:00 PM. At 7:00 PM the classroom would be packed with parents, grandparents, friends, neighbors and, of course, children. I generally gave a short welcome and introduced the first class to make its contribution. Each class had about five-minutes for its part in the program. Following the class presentations, we played "Christmas Bingo." (I don't know about other bingo games, but this one was rigged.) Each child had a card which was one of four colors: red, blue, green or yellow. We rigged the drawings so that each child won a prize regardless of the color of his or her card.

Following bingo, I was expected to tell an original Christmas story which involved some animal like a hungry bear from Palomar Mountain, a rabbit who saved some Christmas presents from being stolen or a preschool cat. (The preschool cat story will be repeated in the next chapter.) At the end of the evening, we always sang holiday songs like Jingle Bells, Rudolph the Red Nosed Reindeer and We Wish You a Merry Christmas.

At eight o'clock we served refreshments and sent everyone home. This schedule seemed to work out well for everyone, including Bob. We never knew what he was going to do or where he was going to be. After all, it was HIS school and he could do as he pleased. When the classes made their presentations, Bob just might be up there lying at their feet. When bingo was being played, he would wander around collecting a few pats here and there. When it was time for the children to leave, he would sit in the classroom waiting for a good night pat until the last person left.

We usually followed this routine, except for the year we used Bob in the Christmas story. On this occasion, by seven o'clock the room was packed and Bob had done his duty of greeting as many parents and children as possible. Alma then went out and grabbed Bob and took him to the back office where he was confined for the entire program. Needless to say, he was not a happy camper. He could hear the children singing and he knew he was missing out on something, so he put up a howl. When the children squealed as they won a bingo prize, he was yelping and begging to be let out of the room.

We changed the order of the activities this year and had the holiday songs prior to the original story. Just before I walked up the stairs to the landing to tell the story, Alma came and whispered that Bob "was in a snit and fit to be tied." She hoped that he would not be so angry that he would not cooperate at the end of the story.

I climbed the stairs and took a big breath before starting the Christmas story featuring Bob, the preschool cat.

# Chapter 7
## BOB'S CHRISTMAS STORY

As I climbed the stairs to the landing and took a big breath, I looked out over the crowd of parents and children packed in this classroom and wondered what the fire marshal would do should he come by now. I also wondered how Bob would react once we let him out of "jail." All these thoughts had to be pushed out of my mind since I had nearly 200 people waiting for a different kind of Christmas story. The story went like this:

Once upon a time there was a wonderful school in Oceanside, California, called El Camino Preschool. In that school lived a very delightful and unusual cat named Bob. Bob was unusual because he did not have a tail. In fact that is why he was named Bob because his lack of a tail made him look like a bobcat.

Every Christmas Bob would sleep under the Christmas

tree in the pre-kindergarten classroom. The teachers would wrap up empty boxes to look like presents and place them under the tree where Bob slept. One day Bob began thinking about all these presents and wondering if one of them was for him. He really wanted something special this year, so he decided to talk to Miss Jill, the administrative assistant.

Bob said, "Miss Jill, am I going to get a present for Christmas?"

Jill replied, "Yes, Bob. I have several things picked out for you. What would you like? How would you like a can of tuna, a new flea collar or maybe even a catnip mouse?"

Bob said, "Thank you Miss Jill, but what I really want is a long tail like other cats."

Jill said, "Bob that is a tall order. I don't know where to get you a tail and if I did, how could we attach it to your body? No, I really can't get you a long tail. If you decide on one of the three things I have suggested, all you have to do is just give me a little hint."

*(Note to the reader: The idea of Bob having an extra tail was not foreign to the children. Several children had seen a gray cat in the neighborhood with a long tail. At a distance it did look like Bob, so they were convinced that Bob had a tail that he could remove or attach whenever he wanted.)*

Bob then goes to Miss Rita, the lead teacher. "Miss Rita, have I been a good cat this year?"

Miss Rita said, "Yes Bob, you have been a very good cat; in fact, you have been the most wonderful cat in the world."

Bob now was very encouraged, so he asked, "Since I have been a good cat, does this mean that I am going to get a special present this Christmas?"

Miss Rita said, "Bob you are going to get a fabulous present this year. I will see that you will get something that would make any cat's heart leap for joy. Now if you will just give your old pal, Rita, a hint I will see that I can do."

Bob was now getting excited so he blurted out, "The most wonderful thing you could get me would be a long tail so I would look like other cats."

Miss Rita was shocked by this request. She replied, "Bob, there is no way I could obtain a tail for you. I don't even know if there are any for sale. How about a can of tuna or a new flea collar? Many cats would be very happy with a catnip mouse; would you like one?"

Bob said, "No thanks, I really want a long tail. It won't be much of a Christmas if I don't have a long tail like other cats. I think I will go and talk to Miss Alma."

Bob had to hunt all over the school and he finally found Miss Alma in the back office. He said, "Am I the number one preschool cat?"

Miss Alma replies, "Of course you are the number one preschool cat because you are the only preschool cat in all of Oceanside."

"Don't you think that if I am the number one cat that I should look like I am the number one cat?" asked Bob.

Miss Alma was a little puzzled with Bob's questions so she tried to get at the problem by saying, "Bob, you are the best looking cat in all of North County. There is nothing that could make you look any better than you are."

Bob then jumped up on a chair by Miss Alma's desk and cried, "Yes there is……..Yes there is. What would really make me look better would be a nice long tail. Miss Alma will you get me a long tail for Christmas? Please! Please! Please!"

Miss Alma replied, "Bob there is no possible way I could get you a tail. You are really a very good cat and I would be more than happy to buy you a wonderful Christmas present, but there is no way I could get a tail for you. It is just impossible. Now be a good cat and think of something practical like a can of tuna, a new flea collar or even a catnip mouse."

Bob said, "If I can't have a tail, I really don't know what I would want. I will just have to give it some thought."

Bob was now feeling very sad. He walked out to the back play yard and was almost ready to cry when he looked up and saw Roger, one of Santa's most trusted Reindeers, while he was eating grass.

Roger said, "Bob this grass is really good. El Camino has the best grass in all of Oceanside. I think I could eat this grass all day long. It is yummy, yummy, yummy in the tummy."

Bob hardly looked up, he was so very, very sad.

Roger said, "Bob, old buddy, what is the matter with you? You look all bummed out. Is there something I can do to help?"

Bob said, "There is nothing you can do and for that matter there is nothing anyone can do. I am just a miserable old cat who no one loves and no one can help. I just don't know what to do."

Roger could see that Bob was feeling very sorry for himself. He was dejected and looked quite pitiful. So Roger said, "Hey, maybe I could help. Tell your old buddy what is wrong."

Bob just exploded, "I want a tail for Christmas and no one understands what it is like to be a cat with no tail. I feel like a freak – I feel deformed – I feel just awful. I just wish I had a good friend who understood what I am going through."

Roger said, "You know, maybe I could help. I know someone who just might be able to get you a tail."

Bob immediately felt better, "Who could that be?"

## BOB'S CHRISTMAS STORY

"Santa Claus," said Roger.

"Do you know Santa Claus?" Bob asked, hardly believing his ears.

"Of course I know Santa. I am his number one reindeer and I just talked with him this morning. In fact, if you are of a mind, I will take you to see him right now. If anyone can get you a tail it will be good old Santa," replied Roger.

Bob was now worried. "How in the world can you take me to see Santa? He lives at the North Pole and I have heard that place is several miles north of Oceanside."

Roger replied, "Bob, it is more than just a few miles, but I can go extremely fast and I could get you there in no time FLAT! All you have to do is get on my back and hold on to my horns and I will show you what fast is really like."

So Bob hops on Roger's back, gets a good grip on his horns and says, "Let's go."

Roger then took a big jump and yelled, "Up, up, and away." In no time they were flying toward the North Pole. The wind was so strong that it was burning Bob's eyes and his paws could hardly hold on to the horns.

Bob said to Roger, "Are we there yet?"

Roger replied, "Not yet."

After a minute, Bob asked, "Are we there yet?"

Roger answered, "It will be a little longer."

Bob was getting impatient, 'Are we there yet? I can hardly hold on to your horns."

Roger said, "Almost – yes, there is the North Pole and I see Santa's office building and all the toy shops." Roger coasted down to a very fine landing in about six inches of new snow.

Bob jumped off Roger's back and said, "WOW! What is this white stuff? Whatever it is, it is making my feet hurt."

Now Bob was a California cat and had never seen snow

so he did not know what to expect. He tried lifting one foot and then the other in order to get away from that cold, white stuff. His feet had never been so cold in all his life.

Roger said, "Bob, that white stuff is snow and yes, it is very cold."

Bob wanted to know more about that stuff that was making his feet hurt. So he asked Roger, "Tell me, just what is this snow?"

Roger said, "Snow is water that is frozen....no that is not right because then it would be ice. Snow then is water which is very cold but is not ice. Oh! I don't know how to explain snow. Let's go and see Santa." He called for an elf to bring Bob some snow boots just the right size for cats. Once Bob had put on the snow boots, his feet felt much better.

Bob and Roger walked across the yard to Santa's office and knocked on the door. Someone inside said, "Open the door and come on in. It is too cold to be standing in the snow."

So Bob and Roger went into the office building where Santa was working by looking at long lists of names. He looked up and said, "Who is your little friend, Roger?"

"This is my friend, Bob the Preschool Cat. He has come all the way from Oceanside to ask if you can provide him with a very special Christmas present," replied Roger.

Santa said, "Roger, you are always getting ahead of everything. We can't talk about Christmas presents until we see if Bob deserves a present."

Santa called to one of his elves and asked for a list of all the good cats in Oceanside.

When the elf brought the list, Santa started looking it over. He said, "I just worked on this list this morning and, in fact, I checked it twice to see what cats have been naughty or nice. Let's see.....ah yes....This is the right list all right. All the names are in order so it should be easy to see if Bob is here. The first good cat is Anne, the next one is Alex then Alexis then Betty followed by Bill. Here it is….Bob the Preschool Cat. Hmmmmmmm. There are a few notes about Bob. It says that he has no bad marks – only good marks. It says that all the boys and girls at the El Camino Preschool dearly love him because he is so good and never hurts or bites children."

Santa turned to Bob and said, "From what I see on that list, you will certainly get a present this year. What kind of a present would you like? I can get you a can of tuna, a new flea collar or maybe a catnip mouse?"

Bob was getting worried. He had come all the way from Oceanside and Santa only wanted to provide the same gifts that the staff members at El Camino wanted to give him, so he exclaimed, "NO! NO! NO! I don't want anything like that. You don't understand. Nobody understands. I want a nice long tail like other cats. I feel so deformed that I know no one will ever love me. Please – Please – Please Santa, will you give me a nice long beautiful tail?"

Santa said, "I think that you look just fine. You are a Manx cat and Manx cats are born without a tail so you are normal. Now tell Santa why you want a tail for Christmas."

Bob had been waiting for just this chance, so he said, "If I had a tail then all the boys and girls at the El Camino Preschool will love me."

Santa started laughing. "Ho – Ho – Ho." Then his belly started shaking like a bowl full of jelly. "Bob, you have got it all wrong. People do not love you because of the way you look. People love you because of the way you act. If you are nice and kind to the boys and girls, if you are not mean and if you do not scratch and bite, how can they help but love you? In fact, according to my good cat list you are the best cat in Oceanside and all the children at the El Camino

Preschool adore you."

As Santa was talking, one of the elves came running into the room and whispered something in Santa's ear. Santa looked very intense before turning again to Bob. "Ginger, the elf, just told me that there is a big Christmas party now in progress at the El Camino Preschool. All the boys and girls are waiting for you to come and greet them. You must hurry back to Oceanside because the party is just about over," Santa said. "Roger, be quick and take Bob back to Oceanside as soon as possible."

Bob and Roger ran outside and Bob jumped on Roger's back and immediately fell off in the snow. Roger said, "You are a silly cat, don't you know that you must take off your snow boots before you can ride on a reindeer's back?"

So Bob sat down and took off the snow boots. This time when he jumped on Roger's back, he did not fall off. He grabbed Roger's horns and held on very tightly while the reindeer flew through the air at almost the speed of light. In no time flat Roger landed in the back play yard of the El Camino Preschool. Bob jumped off Roger's back and rushed into the school to see all the boys and girls who were waiting for him.

*****

This is the end of the story that I told to the children on Teddy Bear Night. However, as I was finishing up the story, Alma had gone into the back office and picked up Bob who was a very unhappy camper. She had no idea how he would react, but when I finished the last sentence, she opened the door from the school office where all the children could see Bob and handed him to me.

# BOB'S CHRISTMAS STORY

Bob did not know what to think. He had never been treated so badly since he took over the position as number one cat. However, his eyes just about popped when he saw all the people looking at him. Then he started wiggling and squirming wanting me to put him down. Not knowing what he would do or what to expect, I put him on the floor and waited to see his behavior.

Most cats, put in this position and treated the way Bob had been treated, would have run out of the room and hid. But most cats were not Bob. He ran down the steps from the landing where I stood while telling the story and headed for the first group of children he could see. He then flopped down on his side as all the children reached to touch and pet their hero. After all, Bob had just been to the North Pole and had actually talked with Santa Claus. To Bob, this was wonderful having all the children wanting to pet him at once.

## BOB THE PRESCHOOL CAT

I said, "This concludes our program for this evening. We want to thank you for coming and making Teddy Bear Night a success. If you will note, it is just now eight o'clock, and you still have time to enjoy some refreshments before leaving. There is coffee, punch and tons and tons of cookies available. Good night, everyone."

I don't think anyone listened to what I said. All the children were crowding around Bob. Each child was trying to get as close to Bob as possible so he or she could actually touch the cat who had talked to Santa Claus. By 8:30 there were still more than half of the parents and children in the school – the parents drinking coffee and punch while the children concentrated on the best way to pet a cat.

By 9:00, at least a third of the families were still present and Bob could not have been more pleased with all the attention. At 9:30, I was getting very tired, so I suggested to the staff that we should start putting the chairs and tables back in place so that the few remaining families would take

the hint and go home. It worked. As soon as we started putting the room back together, the remaining parents said good night and left.

It was ten o'clock before everything was back in place and ready for the next school day. I activated the burglar alarm, turned out the lights and locked the door. As Alma and I walked to the car, I said, "Alma, I am very tired. However, I think that this was the most successful Teddy Bear Night we have had. You can always tell how successful an event is by how long it takes parents to leave."

# Chapter 8
## THE PASSING OF BOB

Like humans, cats do not live forever. We knew that one day Bob would no longer be with us, but this was something about which we did not want to think. He was an outside cat. When school closed for the day, he would go and sit on the steps to the business office and wait until it was time to retire to his sleeping area on the roof.

As the owner of the preschool, I was interested in all aspects of the operation. In the evenings, when I needed to go on an errand, I would always go by the school to see if the janitorial staff was doing their job. This is when I would find Bob sitting out in front on the steps waiting and hoping for someone to arrive.

We often discussed the dangers he faced. Several families refused to obey the animal control laws to keep their dogs fenced or leashed. These were big dogs, which did not

## BOB THE PRESCHOOL CAT

like cats. Bob was "street wise." He knew how to protect himself by climbing a tree should a dog become too aggressive. Then, there were coyotes. Yes, we have coyotes in the middle of Oceanside and most have lost their fear of humans. One day I saw a large coyote crossing the bridge between Oceanside and Carlsbad on El Camino Real oblivious to all the traffic. Many families have lost their cats to coyotes and have written letters to the editor of our newspaper complaining about the lack of coyote control.

If it were only one coyote, we thought that Bob could avoid being caught. However, when several coyotes plan an attack, it is difficult for one cat to survive. This was a risk we were forced to take since he was an outside cat and seemed to know the "score."

It was a Friday morning when I received the dreaded call. My wife called me at the college to say that Bob did not show up when the school opened. Several teachers had gone out and called to him, but there was no response. He would always respond with a "Meow" or in cat language, "Here I am," when called. This lack of response made the entire staff very worried.

As soon as possible after the children were settled in their activities, two staff members started searching the neighborhood for Bob. It did not take long. He was found on the grounds of the church next door. From all indications, he was hit by a car in the parking lot and had managed to crawl on the grass where he died. This church had a very large parking lot where teenagers would race their cars. We felt that he could have been hit during a drag race.

Our problem now was how to break the news to the children. It was Friday, so everyone felt it best to wait until Monday. We prepared a letter (The actual letter is reproduced here) to inform the parents so they could handle

## THE PASSING OF BOB

it at home over the weekend, should they desire. The teachers did not feel that they were in any condition to share their grief and could not be at their best for the children.

We were totally unprepared for the reaction to Bob's death. Although the children were saddened by his death, it was the parents who were devastated. We received phone calls, sympathy cards and even flowers from parents expressing their grief at the loss of Bob. The children seemed to be able to cope with losing Bob much better than the parents.

One parent confused Bob with one of the children and called wanting to know when the funeral would be held and where to send flowers.

After finding Bob's body, we were faced with the problem of caring for the remains. My wife, Alma, purchased a large decorated hat box to use as a coffin. We wrapped him in a large towel before placing him in the box. Since Bob spent every evening sitting on the front steps, we felt that his final resting place should be somewhere close. It was finally decided that behind a pine tree in the corner of the front yard would be the only place where he would never be disturbed. I dug a large hole and several of the staff members were present as we said our final good bye to Bob – a cat which had touched the heart of everyone in the school.

In the picture above one can see the steps where Bob sat each evening until it was time to retire to the roof. Under the tree to the left is where Bob is buried.

# Parent's Letter

Dear Parents:

We have always known that there was a possibility that this could happen, but the reality of it is very sad - we have lost our dear little Bob.

Since this is Friday, we want to take advantage of the weekend, and not tell the children until Monday. Naturally all of us teachers are very sad and upset, and we feel we can deal with discussing the situation with the children better on Monday.

We found him in the church yard next door, but we're not sure what happened to him. That is what we will tell the children. We will explain it to them as gently as possible, and try to deal with their questions as best we can. It is important that they have the opportunity to express their sadness.

We feel it is important to be honest with the children and let them know that Bob is indeed gone and he did not just run away. We feel it is not necessary to go into details or speculation as to exactly how he died. If you decide to talk to your child this weekend about our Bob, we would suggest that you tell them we found him in the church yard next door, but are not sure what happened to him.

We know parents and children will be so sad too, and miss Bob. He was such a part of our preschool family.

El Camino Preschool Staff

# Epilogue

My wife and I no longer own and operate the El Camino Preschool. After nearly twenty years, we sold the school to one of our former teachers and her husband, Heike and Richard Burton, who took over the operation of the school on January 1, 2005.

Teenagers can no longer race their cars through the neighborhood church parking lot where Bob was killed. A wrought iron fence with an electronic gate was installed in front of the church. This has effectively curtailed such activities.

The school is still a warm, friendly place which parents, who resist sending their young children to corporate institutions, dearly love. Still there is one thing missing. Now, there is no well-behaved, gentleman cat to meet, greet and welcome children and their parents each morning. However, there is a group of children (many of which are now in college) whose lives were enriched and forever changed by El Camino Preschool and one remarkable cat.

Printed in the United States
147048LV00002B/1/P